A BOOK TO ENTERTAIN YOUR CHILD

PARTY GAMES

Written and compiled by Morag Walker
Illustrated by Andrew Locke and Anne Parsons

This is no ordinary book of party games. It has one exciting difference. Our author has chosen an amusing theme, and follows it through every detail of the children's party. The fun concludes with a party play, to make the event enjoyable and memorable for parents and children alike.

HENDERSON
PUBLISHING PLC
©1995 HENDERSON PUBLISHING PLC

PLAN A PARTY WITH A DIFFERENCE

> **How would you organise the most fantastic party for between 10 and 12 children, aged between seven and nine years of age?**
>
> **Relax; the formula you need is really very simple.**

First, choose a popular theme and lots of fun party games. Then all you need is a party play and appetising theme-shaped food. These main ingredients are all included in this book.

(The theme I have chosen is Space, which is exciting and inspires boys and girls alike.)

A child of any age looks forward eagerly to their birthday party; but for many parents, the thought of arranging a party can be an onerous task. Now, with a little preplanning and simple organisation, the party can be a huge success for all concerned.

The theme is designed to make the whole party an action-packed event.

There is nothing worse than running a party and wondering what to do next!

Children love to act.

Producing the party play will be a main event. The party play included in this book is written on my chosen theme, Space. You can use it, or adapt it as you wish. It can be produced easily, requiring little scenery and few lines to learn. You do not need elaborate props and each child comes ready dressed in their costume.

Towards the end of the party, parents can be invited to watch the final performance, which gives a focus for the whole party, and the play can be recorded on video as a permanent reminder. These parties have always been a huge success with my family and my four children participate to the full.

It must be remembered that the emphasis on the party should be *FUN*. It does not matter if the children are not word perfect when acting in the play (of course, they won't be in the time available). They have come to the party to enjoy themselves.

Suggestions for everything you need to run a successful theme party are included in the pages that follow:

- **Invitations • Script,**
- **Decorations**
- **Director's Notes** as well as plenty of fun
- **Party Games** to play.

The games can be easily adapted to relate to your chosen theme. There is also a design for a special
- **Going Home Certificate**, so that participants have a lasting memory of a great occasion.

I hope your children enjoy the games and this party play as much as mine have. Once you and your children have got hooked on a theme party, you can try other ideas and adapt them yourself. I have included more theme suggestions on pages 45.

You never know, we might be creating tomorrow's great actors and actresses!

PARTY GAMES

Page

YOUR PARTY TIMETABLE

The Party Play is going to take up a large part of the party time, but everybody enjoys playing party games, so it is a good idea, once the guests have arrived and the presents have been opened, to play a selection of games to break the ice and put the guests in the mood for your theme party.

We allowed three hours for the party, which worked very well and gave ample time for opening presents, playing some games and rehearsing the play.

We found that it was better to have the present opening, games and food during the first part of the party, leaving the rest of the time free to practise the play. Allow 20 minutes towards the end of the party to perform the play and invite parents to watch the final performance. It will give the players an incentive to work hard if they know that they will be performing to a 'real' audience.

Decide where the main action is going to take place and remove all breakables and unwanted furniture. You will also need to have all the props ready for the different games and the play in advance. Planning and organising everything in advance does ensure the smooth running of the party.

PARTY INVITATIONS

MAKE YOUR OWN

It is much better to make your own invitations as you can then tailor the wording to suit your own individual party requirements. Part of the excitement of the party is to let your child help with the organisation as much as possible, so start by letting your child assist with the design of the invitation.

A ROLE TO SUIT

In the Space Party Play, each person invited to the party is designated a specific part. Before sending out the invitation, firstly read the script and decide which child would be most suited to a particular role. Good readers, for example, would make excellent narrators. A more shy child might prefer an easier role, like the cat.

Once you have cast your players, decide on an invitation design. If you are using envelopes, buy these first so that you can make the

invitation to fit. Important details to include are:

• The name of the party-giver and the Space theme.

• Costume requirements, saying, for example, "please come dressed as Captain K..." (choosing a well known TV sci-fi figure).

If the children have off-stage roles, such as the narrators or director, ask them to come dressed in a space costume.

Do stress to parents that simple, improvised costumes are all that are expected.

(You don't want your child's friends to miss the party because their mum or dad hasn't time to concoct an elaborate outfit!)

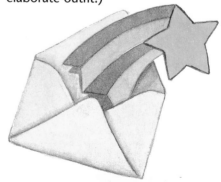

To Kim,

PATRICK'S OUTER SPACE BIRTHDAY PARTY

on Saturday 12th May, at 9 High Street, Fordend, at 2 p.m. until 5 p.m..

Please come dressed as a Space Alien - a simple homemade mask will do fine. Everyone will be dressed up for our special Space Party Play.

Parents are invited to watch us all perform if they come at 4.30 p.m..

R.S.V.P. Tel. 0033 949596

If you have not received a reply from a particular child, it is probably a good idea to contact them to see whether or not they are able to come to the party.

• Invite a parent to watch the play (20 minutes before home time).

• Also include the date and time of the party plus your address and phone number for replies.

Send the invitations out in good time, at least three weeks before the party and keep a list of invited guests to check against as they reply.

Themed invitations could include a space rocket, a planet with dust circle around and a shooting star. Make the invitations bright with coloured card and include lots of glitter, sequins, and silver stars. Party details could be written in gold or silver pens.

The designs below can be copied and used as templates for your Space invitations.

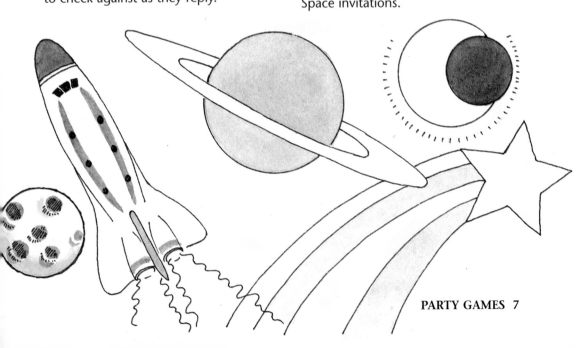

PRIZES TO MATCH YOUR THEME

REWARDS ALONG THE WAY
Games are an essential part of a party, children really look forward to them, and they never tire of the old favourites.

To keep everyone happy as the games progress, it can be a good idea to award small bite-size prizes at frequent intervals. This way, not only the outright winner of the game wins a prize, but competitors who win a round or get a question right can earn a small token prize, too.

SPACE PARTY
Always plan plenty of games because they never last as long as you think and some may not work as well as you hoped.

If you are giving prizes (which are part of the fun), buy a selection of small theme novelties, like space rocket erasers, space soap, space-shaped sweets, and so on. These can be individually wrapped and put in a box, like a Lucky Dip. The winner can then select one out of the box without knowing what it is.

Look out for:
- Stickers
- Shaped sweets
- Individually wrapped nibbles
- Inexpensive modelling clay
- Bubble making kits
- Shaped or coloured balloons
- Stationery items
- Cereal packet novelties

JUNGLE PARTY

Tropical mix - wrapped in green tissue paper, like a large leaf. Available loose from many fruiterers or in packets from supermarkets and some grocers.

Sun-dried banana pieces chopped, or a slice wrapped in rice paper wrappers, like cigars.

Everlasting flowers - a few flower-heads on short wires, pressed safely into Plasticine will make an exotic keepsake for a window sill or bookshelf.

A coconut would make an excellent first prize for someone to take home.

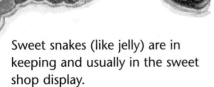

Sweet snakes (like jelly) are in keeping and usually in the sweet shop display.

Stationery items, like parrot erasers or pencil sharpeners, are very appealing.

PIRATES

Small plastic toys, like a skull key ring or pencil eraser, are just the thing.

Novelty confectionery also produces some grisly shapes to fit the bill here.

• A balloon, with a Skull and Crossbones painted in felt pen, is sure to please.

• A parrot sticker, dispensed from a long sheet, makes a popular small gift.

NURSERY RHYME CHARACTERS (OR PANTO)

Chocolate coins - a single coin is an ideal token prize, e.g., Pass the Parcel.

Christmas tree fancies, like sugar mice, can often fit the theme.

Small chocolate eggs (from Christmas and Easter stocks) are much treasured at other times of the year.

DECORATIONS

A few very simple decorations around the room will highlight the theme of your party and delight your young guests immediately

FOR A SPACE THEME PARTY
If you use the Space theme, this is easy and effective. Cut out cardboard stars and moons and cover with silver foil. Hang these up, on cotton threads, together with silver and black balloons to give the room a feeling of outer space.

FOR A WILD WEST PARTY
Cut-outs are effective for this theme, too: **Cacti,** on green card or painted newspaper, are simple to draw and look just the part.

OTHER THEMES:
For a Nursery Rhyme Party
Cut-out pink and white clouds can be hung on cotton from the ceiling or wall lamps.

A cut-out of a fairytale castle (perhaps copy the shape from a Disney advertisement) will make a good centrepiece high on a wall.

A town sign, strung between two tall posts, reading Dodge City or Coffin Creek, can set the scene. Again, cut from newspaper and paint with poster paints.

FOR A JUNGLE PARTY

Large palm leaves and fronds can be cut from newspaper, painted green and fixed to windows, walls and doors with Blu-Tack, which shouldn't spoil the paintwork.

Painted seagull feathers stuck into Plasticine can give an effect of exotic birds amongst the foliage.

FOR A PIRATES PARTY

A clean piece of garden netting, hung from the corners of the ceiling, is good. Small flags, shells, an old alarm clock, toy parrot, even a toy crocodile are all evocative of J. M. Barrie's well known pirates in *Peter Pan*.

Black sugar paper Jolly Roger, flags with skull and crossbones drawn in white chalk or white paint, are a must. Cut out an anchor, too, and fix it to the back of the door.

A rope, coiled in the corner, can look very nautical.

FOR AN UNDERWATER PARTY

This isn't as strange as it might sound. The theme could be Deep Sea, Water Nymphs or one of many watery ideas.

A collection of shells and pebbles in clusters about the room will set the scene.

Bubbles, cut to various sizes, from glossy blue pages from old magazines, can appear to float to the surface, up the walls.

If you have a spare roll of plain wallpaper, children will love painting waves onto it. This can simply stand up against the skirting board, like a frieze, if you prefer not to stick anything onto the walls themselves.

GAMES FOR ANY CHILDREN'S PARTY

You can adapt most games to fit any theme. To see how simple this is, see the selection of games on pages 18 which I have adapted and tested for our Space theme party.

BLIND MAN'S BUFF

One child is chosen to have their eyes covered with a scarf, so they cannot see. This 'blind man' is led to stand in the centre of the room.

(The room should be free of delicate objects that might be accidentally tipped up or broken during the chase which follows.)

This is a traditional part of the game which is often forgotten:

The other players ask, *"How many horses has your father got?"*, to which the 'blind man' replies *"Three"*.

"What colours are they?" players ask.

The blind man replies *"Black, white and grey"*.

All the players chant at the blind man *"Turn around three times and catch who you may."*

The blindfolded player spins around three times, and then has to catch one of the other players, who dodge around the room. The first to be caught is the next to be blindfolded.

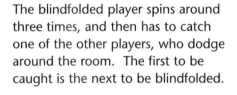

When a player is caught, they should keep perfectly quiet, while the blind-folded player tries to identify who they have caught.

SIMON SAYS

This is an excellent game for all ages, and a good one to get things going.

One child plays the role of 'Simon', and stands facing everyone else. Simon gives a series of commands to be followed by the group. However, the group only does as they are told if they hear "Simon says".

So, if the group hear *"Simon says put your hands on your head"*, players must do so. If, however, the instruction is given as simply *"Put your hands on your head"*, then any player who does so is out of the game.

Instructions should flow thick and fast, and very soon, players will fall by the wayside, eager to carry out the instruction and forgetting whether Simon said so, or not!

Instructions could include:
Put your right arm up.
Bend your knees.
Fold your arms.
Put your finger on your lips.
Stand on one leg.
Clap your hands.
Stop!
Simon says 'Stop'.

NORTH SOUTH EAST WEST

Label the four corners of the room North, South, East and West - you could write the words on large pieces of paper and pin them to the walls.

All players stand in the middle, and an adult calls out one of the compass points. Everyone has to run to the right corner - the last one there is out of the game each time.

ON AND OFF

Another lively elimination game to warm things up.

Spread an old blanket on the floor. Nominate a leader to be in charge of shouting orders. Whatever they command, the pack must *disobey*. If they say *"Everyone on the blanket"*, players should stand off it. *"Everyone off the blanket"* should send players clambering onto it.

Anyone who makes a mistake or hesitates for too long is 'out'.

SPIDER'S WEB

If you choose this game, it is best played as your guests arrive.

Tie balls of wool to chocolate or candy bars - one for each of your guests. Hide the goodies and unravel the wool around the room - over and under furniture, round door handles, and in and out of all the other balls of wool as you go along.

Let the children into the room to unravel their wool. They will eventually get to their reward, climbing amongst their friends as they go! For younger children, a less complicated route can be laid in a different coloured wool.

SQUEAK, PIGGY, SQUEAK

The player who is 'it' is blindfolded and given a cushion. They are turned around three times, then all the other players sit around them in a circle. 'It' has to find a player, put the cushion on their lap, and sit on it. He calls out "Squeak, Piggy, Squeak" and the player squashed underneath must squeak loudly.

If the person who is 'it' can identify the 'piggy' then they swap places. If not, then 'it' finds someone else to sit on. Whenever someone new takes over as 'it', all the players change places in the circle after the blindfold is in place.

MUSICAL STATUES

Play some lively dance music for this one. Everyone has to dance along until the music stops. Then, players must *freeze*. If you detect any movement from a player before the music starts again, that player is out.

HUNT THE THIMBLE

This game should be confined to one room. One person should hide the chosen object whilst the others are out of the room. In place of a thimble, use a marble, or an empty matchbox. Make sure everyone knows what the hidden object is.

PAIR THEM UP

Players must find pairs of small objects - cotton reels, pencils, stamps, paperclips, etc.

One of each pair is put into a bag, and the others hidden around the room or the entire house. Explain to players that items will be hidden in unusual places - so a paperclip in the desk drawer won't be the hidden item they are looking for.

To play, each person is given a selection of items to 'pair up', by finding the identical twin. There probably won't be a winner in this game as everyone will find all, or most of their items.

Call everyone back into the room to hunt. The 'hider' can help a little - telling the searchers if they are 'getting warm' (when they are near the object), or 'getting colder' (moving away from it).

The first to find it is the winner, and hides it again when the others leave the room.

Items you could use:

- shoe laces • buttons
- tangerines • egg cups
- gloves, socks • bookends
- ribbons • spoons • candles
- Xmas tree decorations
- matchboxes • paper cake cases
- corks

MATCHBOX RACE

Divide young players into teams. Give the first person of each team the outside cover of a matchbox. On 'go', place the box on their nose. This has to be passed, nose to nose, down the line of players. No hands are allowed, unless the box is dropped, when it starts from the front again.

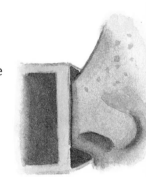

When the last player gets the box safely, they must run to the other end and start passing down again - until the original leader is back at the front of the queue.

DETECTIVE

This is a quieter game, useful to calm any over excitement.

Players form a circle, with one player in the middle, blindfolded.

The players in the circle quietly swap places, with one leaving the room. The blindfolded 'detective' may then remove the blindfold to look around and try to work out who has left the room.

DONKEY'S TAIL

Draw a donkey, with no tail, onto a large sheet of paper. The outline given here may help, if, like most of us, you've never drawn a donkey before!

Fix the picture to a noticeboard or flat piece of wood. (If played outside, a fence or outside wall will do.)

Each player in turn is blindfolded and given the donkey's tail - a piece of frayed string with a drawing pin through the end. The player should then try to pin the tail where they guess it should go - not easy! Mark their attempt with a cross and their initials, then blindfold the next person to have a go.

The winner is the player who got nearest - it's surprising how wild some of the guesses will be.

TASTEBUD TEST

This should be prepared in advance, away from prying eyes.

Prepare several cups with small measures of different things to drink. You could use cola, diet cola, cold tea, different fruit juices, soup, mineral water, tap water, soda water, lemon juice, cold coffee - or any other safe concoctions you can think of.

A blindfold makes the test more 'scientific', though it isn't essential. Each player is given their own spoon to test from each cup. Keep score of the answers on paper. The player who identifies most liquids correctly wins the game.

SPACE PARTY GAMES

Every party needs a little music and for some of these games, it's essential.

You may have your own ideas of 'outer space' music; something like an instrumental recording by Mike Oldfield (of Tubular Bells fame) would be highly appropriate to use for an atmospheric background throughout these activities.

SPACESHIP

During the weeks before the party, start collecting sweet wrappers, yogurt pots, cardboard tubes from kitchen roll, cereal boxes, pieces of foil or anything else that can be used for building. Ask the children to make a spaceship using anything from the pile of things you have collected. Provide sticky tape and a tube or two of paper glue, to help the builders construct the spaceship. This is a good first game and people can join in as they arrive.

MUSICAL STARS
Based on Musical Chairs

Cut out a number of large stars in silver foil, one for each child playing. An adult operates the music controls of a radio or hi-fi. Children parade, to the music, like astronauts, around the room until suddenly, the music stops. At that moment, everyone has to sit on a star. After the first short musical round, decrease the number of stars. The child without a star to perch on when the music stops is out of the game. Remove one more star each round. Last child with a star to sit on wins.

FIND THE SECRET FORMULA FOR A NEW SPACE ROCKET

Where has the secret formula been hidden? Draw a large space picture with rockets, planets, stars, and moons.

Get everyone to stick a dot (with their initials on), where they think the secret formula is hidden. Secretly mark the hiding place on the back of the picture before the game starts. A prize for the nearest dot.

> **Note:** 4 pieces of A4 paper taped together gives a good size picture for players to gather round.

> **Note:** It is fairer if the person controlling the music turns their back to the players.

SPIN THE FLYING SAUCER

The children sit in a circle and are numbered from one upwards. A person is chosen to spin the saucer (a dinner plate) and calls out a number. The person who has that number must catch the plate before it stops spinning. If they do not then they are out. Anyone calling a number of someone who is already out also becomes out.

BLINDFOLDED SPACE OBSTACLE COURSE

A simple obstacle course is laid out from the door of the room to a finishing point. The obstacles might be a cushion, a pile of books, a basket, someone lying across the course, or whatever. Volunteers offer to walk the course blindfold, after having carefully studied the course.

The volunteers all leave the room and are brought in one by one and set off on the course whilst everyone gives helpful advice, such as "Look out!" *"Move left " "Careful, you will stand on him."*

But, while the volunteers are out of the room, all the obstacles have been removed! When the volunteers have their blindfolds removed, their expression, when they realise there was nothing on the floor adds to the amusement.

MAGIC MEMORY GAME

Bring a tray into the room filled with items that fit into the space theme. These could include a toy rocket, a toy astronaut, a piece of rock, star and moon pastry cutters or card cut-outs, silver foil, a saucer, a space gun and so on. The children are given about 60 seconds to look at the items. They then have to write down as many as they can. The person who guesses the most is the winner.

SPACE WALK
(5-6 year olds may find this difficult)

Divide children into two teams and stand half of each team at either end of the room.

Give one child from each team two bricks. These children have to race to the other end of the course using the bricks as stepping stones and moving them along! They must not step on the floor. If they do, they must start from the beginning again. At the other end, another team member takes over and races back. Keep going until everyone has had a go.

The first team to finish is the winner.

PICKING UP SPACE MONEY
Tell your guests that they can win an intergalactic ten-pence coin if they can pick it up off the floor. Ask for a volunteer. Stand him or her with their back to the wall, heels touching the skirting board. Then put a ten-pence coin within two feet of his or her toes. If they can pick it up without moving their heels from the wall and without bending their knees they can keep it!

SPACE HOOP-LA

Cut out hoops of stiff cardboard and throw them over mini bags of space sweets; include flying saucers, gold stars and so on. (Well-known confectioners make various mini chocolate bars which have space-like names.)

> **Note:** Saucepan lids make ideal templates to draw around for the hoops

CRASH ROCKETS

The players all dance around in a circle to lively music. When the leader calls 'rockets sit down in threes' (or 'twos' or in 'fours'), everyone rushes to get into a group of three (or whatever) sitting on the floor. Those who are last to sit down or who are left out of a group are out. The last pair left in the game are the winners.

PASS THE SPACE PARCEL

Children of all ages love this game and never seem to lose interest in it.

To give a space theme, wrap the parcel in layers of silver foil or paper and put glitter or coloured stars or space sweets between each layer, so that every child has an opportunity of winning something. Sit the children in a tight circle and choose some lively music which will encourage the children to pass the parcel at a good speed. When the music stops, a layer is removed.

Try to organise the music so that each child has a chance of removing a layer of paper.

SLEEPING ASTRONAUTS

This is an excellent contrast, after a series of lively games, when 'enthusiasm' is running high. Either choose someone to be 'it' or, alternatively be 'it' yourself.

All the children become sleeping astronauts, lying flat on their backs on the floor, as still as possible with straight faces.

The 'it' person goes around trying to make the sleeping astronauts laugh. 'It' can do anything, like pulling funny faces, or telling jokes, but without actually touching.

Anyone found laughing is out. The last astronaut left in is 'it' in the next round.

RING AROUND VENUS

Sit all the children in a circle and thread a ring onto a piece of string long enough to go round the circle of children.

Choose one child to sit in the middle. The children in the circle hold the string with their hands curled over it, fingers forwards so that it is difficult to see where the ring is.

The children pass the ring around the circle as quickly as possible and the child in the middle has to guess where it is. The children can try and confuse the child guessing by pretending to pass the ring along even when they have not got it.

The child passing the ring when the guesser gets it right becomes the next guesser.

STUCK IN SPACE

This is a very energetic game which the children really enjoy. Choose a person to be 'it'.

He or she rushes around trying to catch as many children as possible. When a child is caught, he or she has to stand still with legs apart, until released by one of the other children who has to crawl between the legs of the child 'stuck in space'.

Put a time limit on this game so that several children have a turn at being 'it'.

ALIENS AND SPACEMEN

Children of any age find this very funny, and nobody needs to be a great artist to participate.

Each person is given a piece of paper and a pencil.

Firstly, get everyone to draw the face of an alien or spaceman at the top of the page and fold the paper over so that no one can see what has been drawn. They must, however, leave the lines of the neck showing, so the second person knows where to draw the figure, including arms if necessary, to the waist.

Once again fold the paper over to hide the body, leaving just the ends of the waist visible.

The third person draws the figure to the knees and folds it over and finally, the last person draws to the feet. Everyone folds down the whole drawing once more and passes it on to the fifth person to open.

The person to open the drawing can then have the pleasure of giving the creature a name!

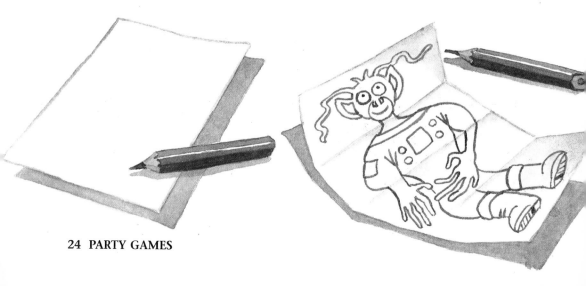

ALIEN'S FOOTSTEPS

Ask one of the children to stand facing the wall and put all the other children at the opposite end of the room. They must creep up on the Alien, but he or she can turn round at any time. Anyone the Alien catches moving must go back to the start. The first person to get close enough to touch the Alien on the shoulder becomes the next Alien.

SPACE WINK MURDER

One child is chosen to be the space detective and is sent out of the room whilst all the rest are put into a circle. While the 'space detective' is away, the organiser chooses someone to be the murderer.

The detective is then invited back into the room. The murderer has to wink at other children in the room.

(Children should be gently reminded that only the murderer is allowed to wink.)

Those winked at have to fall to the ground and play dead. The child who has just been away from the room has to guess who is the murderer.

After five people have been murdered the 'space detective' has to guess who is the murderer.

Each team has a wide-necked jar or small bowl. The team members take it in turn to stand over the jar and drop their stars, one by one, into the jar from waist height.

STAR JARS

This is a team game that requires quite a lot of concentration.

Divide the children into two teams and give each team member half a dozen silver or gold stars.

The team with the most stars safely in the jar is the winner.

Use packets of small stick-on stars, or larger stars, easier for younger children, cut from coloured card, or plain card and sprinkled in glitter.

ALIENS AND MARTIANS

For this game you need a number of small objects such as hats, gloves, scarfs, paper cups and so on. Each team has an equal number of objects. Boundary lines are drawn at either end of the playing area and the teams, the Aliens and Martians, store their property behind their boundary line.

KEEP THE PLANET IN SPACE

Blow-up and decorate two balloons to resemble planets. Sort out two teams and give each team a balloon.

The object of the game is for each team to collect their opponent's property. A player can only take one item at a time but then goes back to his or her own home base without being caught. If a player is captured, they then stay in the enemy base until rescued by being tagged. If a player is rescuing another, they cannot also take any booty on that turn.

The game finishes when one team has all or nearly all the other team's property.

When the organiser starts the game each team has to throw up its balloon and keep it there by blowing it. If anyone touches the balloon or lets it drop they are out.

The winning team is the one to keep the balloon in the air the longest.

SPACE PARTY FOOD

The party food is another exciting aspect of the birthday and the children look forward eagerly to an array of appetising dishes. With my children, I found that at a certain age, they went from just picking at bits and pieces to consuming vast quantities of food, and without exception descended on the food table like a plague of locusts, devouring everything in sight!

I try to offer a wide selection of both sweet and savoury dishes including fresh fruit and raw vegetables with a dip. The cake is always the highlight of the party tea. There are numerous books on the subject giving some excellent design ideas, or if time is limited, you can have one specially made by a local bakery.

I'm not an expert cake decorator but have always enjoyed making my children's birthday cakes. With many shops and supermarkets now supplying a wide array of interesting cake decorations, colours and icing, it is great fun to have a go at making it yourself.

THE CAKE

For a space theme you could try making an Alien, Robot, Space Station, or a Space Rocket. If you decide on the rocket, you could add indoor sparklers at the bottom which will give a dramatic effect.

To make the cake part of the Rocket, buy two Swiss rolls, one larger than the other and fix them on top of each other with butter icing.

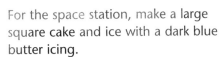

Add an ice-cream cone for the nose and ice-cream wafers at the base for fins. Cover the whole with fondant icing, moulding to shape and decorate with sweets, or pipe on coloured icing.

Finally, stick the sparklers at the base of the cake.

For the space station, make a large square cake and ice with a dark blue butter icing.

Cut up 5 ice-cream cones and colour with a thick blue icing sugar paste, leave to dry. When dry, position on the cake to resemble craters.

Make rough mountain peaks in two of the corners with the dark blue butter icing.

Select a couple of small space buggy or rocket toys and put on cake and finish by making a path with silver balls.

THE PARTY FOOD

To add to the fun, theme food can be labelled with home-made flags on cocktail sticks.

Star Sandwiches - butter and spread brown or white bread with a selection of fillings (Marmite, jam, peanut butter and so on). Cut out star shapes with large star shaped cutter.

Unidentified Flying Sandwiches - Use small bread rolls and fill with slices of salami slightly larger than the bun. Pipe small blobs of cream cheese all around the outside edge and then attach a sweetcorn kernel to each one, to represent windows.

Rocket Stick - Slice French stick longways and fill with tuna, mayonnaise and lettuce. Put back together and add toast triangles at the back to represent fins. Pipe cream cheese windows on the nose of the rocket. Cut up into slices when ready to serve.

Martian Dip (with crudities)
Make dip with sour cream or yogurt, softened cream cheese, mint and finely chopped cucumber. Cut up small sticks of vegetables such as carrot, cucumber, green peppers, and use with dip.

Moon Rocks - Melt 200 gms block of milk chocolate add 2 tablespoons of golden syrup and then mix in sufficient rice crispies to absorb the chocolate and syrup mixture. Spoon into individual cake cases and leave to set.

Planet Pizza Tartlets - For Filling; fry an onion until soft. Add tomato puree, roughly chopped tomatoes, basil, seasoning and drop of sugar. Simmer for 30 minutes until mixture is thick. Roll out shortcrust pastry and cut out and line 12 tartlet tins. Place a heaped teaspoon of mixture in each case. Top with cheese and garnish with black olive.

Alien's Eyeballs - Skin and remove pips from red grapes. Put into glass jar and add red food colouring. Shake well.

Northern Light Fruit Kebabs - Using a cocktail stick spike several different coloured pieces of cut-up fruit, for example, banana, kiwi, cherry, melon, red grapes, orange and so on.

Lost in Space Jelly - Mash up dark coloured jelly and sprinkle with silver balls to represent twinkling stars.

Martian Fizz - Frost the rim of transparent plastic glasses with egg white and then dip into caster sugar. Pour in Limeade (add extra green food colouring if desired) then drop in a spoonful of vanilla ice-cream. Sprinkle coloured hundreds and thousands on top.

THE PARTY PLAY

STAR JARS

THE CHARACTERS

STORYTELLER (2)

OLD TOM

PLUTO (THE CAT)

CAPTAIN KRIK

FRIENDLY ALIEN

ASTRONAUT

TV ANNOUNCER

UNFRIENDLY ALIEN

DIRECTOR OF PLAY

PERFORMING IDEAS

The number of performers in this play can vary to suit the number of your young guests. If, for example, there are more children invited to the party than there are parts, then you can create additional characters by increasing the number of customers visiting the shop and writing in additional lines accordingly. As a guide-line this particular play is best for approximately 10 to 12 children.

The play is very adaptable and the characters can be played equally well by either boys or girls. There is no reason why Captain KRIK cannot be played by a girl or the cat played by a boy! In fact this could be more fun.

You will need to photocopy the script to match the number of characters performing in the play.

STAGE DIRECTION

The Director of the play is very important as the children need to relate well together. You might decide that one of the children would be a suitable person to direct the play. Alternatively, you might prefer to take charge yourself, as you will probably know the children quite well. If a child is going to direct, it is best for an adult to be around to help out generally with suggestions and to ensure the smooth running of the event.

• When you are ready for rehearsal, it is a good idea for the children to sit down in a circle and read their lines aloud together, enabling them to get a feel for the story.

• Follow this by starting to act out the play, sorting out exits and entrances, movements and use of props.

• The Director and spare members of the cast organise the scenery, props and lighting.

• At the same time, speaking characters can sit down on their own in order to familiarise themselves with their lines.

• Depending on the time factor, when everything is ready, it would then be useful to have at least one or two full dress rehearsals with props before your audience arrives.

THE CHARACTERS

The children should arrive at the Party in their designated costumes. Have some face paints ready to add to the character of the faces.

Old Tom could have dark lines drawn on his face to show age and his hair greyed with talcum powder and then jelled to stand up, giving a mad professor appearance. A pair of large spectacles and a long white coat would also look good.

The Friendly Alien If a girl is to play this part, she could wear an all-in-one leotard with a glittered star head band on her forehead and a glitter belt around her waist. Apply green face paint to the face and glitter face paint around the eyes.

Unfriendly Alien A simple costume for the unfriendly alien would be a dark coloured track suit. Make a black stocking mask by cutting out mouth and eye holes and decorate with dark coloured paper shapes. Black stockings on the hands also decorated with coloured paper would finish the effect.

The Astronaut A light coloured track suit with a wide belt could be used for the astronaut. Spray a bathing hat and rubber gloves silver and tape foil dishes to the side of the cap. Trim a pair of Wellington boots with foil and sticky tape.

To make a space back pack, cut out a small cardboard box and cover with foil.

Attach webbing to box and tie on to astronaut.

The Cat Make a mask out of black card and use pipe cleaners for whiskers. Black gloves, a black tracksuit with a black tail (a black stocking stuffed with paper) would make a suitable cat.

Captain KRIK For Captain KRIK, obtain an all-in-one jump suit. Make belt to contain communicator and weapon and attach braid around cuffs and collar.

> **Note:** Other characters in the play such as the narrators and TV announcer should also be asked to arrive at the party dressed in a space theme costume.

Props

- Table
- Very Large Screwdriver
- Magic Jam Jars
- Cheese on Saucer
- Items to be Repaired
- Case to contain Rent Money
- Tools
- Various broken items waiting for repair
- Television - large cardboard box cut out like a TV with picture and knobs painted on.

Sound Effects

- Door bell ring
- Star Trek Music
- Space music
- Loud crashing noise (announcing arrival of Unfriendly Alien)

SET THE SCENE:

- **Preparing the stage:** first decide where the audience will be seated, where the actors will exit and enter and where to position the repair shop.

- **Simple props:** Repair Shop - a small table is sufficient. The table may be filled with any household repair items. For example, broken toys, tools, upturned bikes, tyres and of course, anything with a space feel would be most acceptable.

A sign saying "Old Tom's Magic Repair Shop" would set the scene.

Magic Star Jars : you will need enough to house both the items being repaired and for the nuts and bolts when things go wrong in the magic star jars. To make the star jars obtain some large jam jars and either paint them silver or, alternatively, cover them with silver foil.

Items to be repaired : space telescope, space time watch, and a magnetic space belt. But these could be easily replaced by other items that you have to hand and which will fit the stage space restrictions.

LIGHTING

Spot lights, if available, add atmosphere to the play. Main lights or side lights can be used instead.

When scenes change the lighting can be switched down to denote a change.

THE PERFORMANCE

By now, the children will be full of excitement!

• As your audience arrives, seat them down (or stand them at the back of the room) and position your actors so that they are ready for their cues. When everything is ready, the Director of the play can announce the title of the play saying (birthday child's name) [John Smith's] Theatre Company has pleasure in presenting "Star Jars".

• Play some space-type music and then go straight into the first scene. The Storyteller should sit by the side of the stage where they can be clearly audible and the Director will need to be fairly close to the stage so that he or she can follow the script and give stage prompts when necessary.

At the end of the performance, all actors and the Director should come onto the stage together to give a bow and receive applause.

STAR JARS PLAY Script Page 1

OPENING SCENE

Old Tom's repair shop on the moon. Rows of star jars each containing lots of nuts and bolts. Table with broken toys, tools and so on. Old Tom is busy at the table repairing a broken toy with a very large screwdriver. His cat, Pluto, is by his side.

STORYTELLER 1: It was the year 2090, the planet Earth was completely ruled by computers and everything was mechanised and disposable. There were no more shops or towns. If you wanted to buy something you pressed a button and 'hey presto' the item appeared down a chute in your home.

The trouble with this system was that if something became broken you could not get it repaired, you just threw it away. As you can imagine the pile of rubbish grew and grew until finally the Earth people had to build another planet just for their junk!

STORYTELLER 2: Old Tom, was very old (over 100 years old in fact), and did not like all this throwing away.
He remembered the days when you mended precious toys and

cars and washing machines. So, being an old engineer, he decided to move from Earth with his cat Pluto, and go and live on the moon. He decided to live on the moon because, as we all know, the moon is made of cheese, and his cat Pluto only ate cheese!

Old Tom had been living happily on the moon for 20 years. He had opened a very special repair shop that repaired anything and everything that you could think of.

Sometimes Old Tom would repair things with his huge screwdriver, but sometimes, he would put special items in Star Jars and these would be mended by magic.

OLD TOM: Well, Pluto. Are you ready for your breakfast of lovely cheese?

PLUTO: Meow, Meow.
(Cat rubs against Old Tom)

OLD TOM: I will just finish repairing this toy space car for little Felix.

STAR JARS PLAY Script Page 2

(Old Tom puts some cheese on a saucer for Pluto, when the door bell rings and an Astronaut walks into the shop)

ASTRONAUT: 'Morning Old Tom, how are you? Busy I see.

(Astronaut walks around the shop as he talks looking around)

OLD TOM: Oh yes, Oh yes, so busy. I work from morning until night repairing all the things people do not want to throw away.

ASTRONAUT: Well, do you think you could repair my special space telescope? My mother gave it to me when I first became an astronaut, and it is very dear to me. I would hate to throw it away.

OLD TOM: Yes, no problem. Leave it with me and it will be ready tomorrow.

ASTRONAUT: Oh, thank you. I have to go on a trip to Mars today, but I should be back tomorrow morning. Goodbye.

(Astronaut leaves the shop)
(Old Tom picks up the telescope)

OLD TOM: *(To Pluto)* Well, Pluto, I think this requires a special repair job. I will put this in a magic star jar.

PLUTO: *(Nodding his head)* Meow, Meow.

(Old Tom puts telescope in magic star jar)

(Bell rings again announcing a new customer. In walks Captain KRIK, sound effect - space music)

CAPTAIN KRIK: Good morning, Old Tom.

OLD TOM: Good morning, Captain KRIK. What an honour.

CAPTAIN KRIK: I was wondering, Old Tom, could you mend my special space time watch? My dear friend Dr. Spank gave it to me when I became Captain of the Escapade. He would be most disappointed if I had to throw it away.

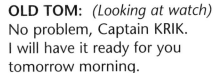
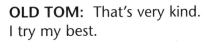

STAR JARS PLAY Script Page 3

OLD TOM: *(Looking at watch)* No problem, Captain KRIK. I will have it ready for you tomorrow morning.

CAPTAIN KRIK: That will be great. I am just going on a mission to visit a new interstellar space station so I should be back tomorrow. Thank you and goodbye. Beam me up, Paddy.
(Captain KRIK leaves the shop)

OLD TOM: *(To Pluto)* Well, Pluto, we must make sure that Captain KRIK's space watch is mended well. *(Picks up watch)* We must put this in one of the magic star jars. *(Old Tom puts the watch into another star jar)*

(Door bell rings again and in walks a Friendly Alien)

FRIENDLY ALIEN: Good morning. Are you 'Old Tom'?

OLD TOM: Yes, that's me.

FRIENDLY ALIEN: I am from the planet Gamma and I heard from a good friend on Earth that you are very clever, and can repair anything.

OLD TOM: That's very kind. I try my best.

FRIENDLY ALIEN: Do you think you could repair my magnetic space belt? It was given to me by the ruler of my planet for saving his daughter's life, so it is very special and I would hate to have to throw it away.

OLD TOM: *(Examining the space belt)* No problem. Leave it with me. It should be ready tomorrow.

FRIENDLY ALIEN: I am so pleased. I am just popping to Zeon, but will be back tomorrow. Thank you. Goodbye.

(Old Tom puts the magnetic space belt into one of the magic star jars and then returns to his table to repair a toy with his large screwdriver)

OLD TOM: *(To Pluto)* My Pluto, we *are* busy today. My magic star jars are nearly all full up.

PLUTO: *(Nodding his head)* Meow, Meow.

(A loud crash is heard outside the shop, announcing the arrival of the Unfriendly Alien)

OLD TOM: *(Looking very startled)* What was that crash Pluto?

PLUTO: Meow! *(Crawls under the table)*

(Door opens. In storms an unfriendly alien)

STORYTELLER 1:
The Unfriendly Alien, from the Planet Dork is one of the nastiest inhabitants of the solar system. He robs and steals and enjoys making everybody very unhappy.

OLD TOM: *(Very nervously)* Yes, c-c-can I h-h-help you?

ALIEN: *(In a deep frightening voice)* Are you 'Old Tom'?

OLD TOM: Y-y-yes.

UNFRIENDLY ALIEN: How long has your repair shop been on the moon?

OLD TOM: Well umm, well, 20 years I think.

UNFRIENDLY ALIEN: *(In a nasty roaring voice)* This is my planet and you now owe me seventeen million space pounds in rent. And I want it NOW.

OLD TOM: But I have not got seventeen million space pounds. All I have is my shop and star jars.

UNFRIENDLY ALIEN: *(Pointing his finger at Old Tom)* I don't want to hear your snivelling excuses. I WANT MY RENT. *(In very loud voice)*

OLD TOM: *(Shaking his head)* But this is impossible. I have no money.

UNFRIENDLY ALIEN: Then you better get some. If you do not pay my money by next week, I will come back and eat you and your fleabag cat. In the meantime, I put a curse on this shop. *(Laughs nastily)* HA, HA, HA, HA.

(Unfriendly Alien leaves the shop)

STAR JARS PLAY Script Page 5

STORYTELLER 2: Poor Old Tom. *(Tom sinks into a chair in despair)* What will he do? How can he find all that money?

(Old Tom shakes his head, and the cat puts its head on his lap)

(Old Tom stands up and goes towards his magic star jars)

OLD TOM: Well Pluto, I better mend these things we had today. Let me say the magic words. APPLE DAPPLE STEW, MAKE EVERYTHING LIKE NEW. *(Old Tom taps all the magic star jars)*

STORYTELLER 1: Poor Old Tom is very tired after the upsetting visit from the Unfriendly Alien. So he goes to bed hoping that all will be well the next day.

(Old Tom leaves the stage)

SCENE 2

STORYTELLER 2: Next day Old Tom is in his shop working at his repair table when his customers from the day before return for their repaired goods.

(Old Tom is sitting at his repair table, Pluto is by his side)

(Door bell rings and in walks the Astronaut)

ASTRONAUT: Good morning Old Tom. Is my space telescope repaired yet?

STORYTELLER 1: Old Tom picks up a star jar and tips it out on the table. But what a shock. Instead of the mended space telescope, a lot of nuts and bolts pour out of the star jar.

ASTRONAUT: *(Very angrily)* What's happened? Where is my space telescope?

STORYTELLER 2: Old Tom shakes his head sadly. The Unfriendly Alien's curse had come true. Old Tom promises the Astronaut that he will try again and asks him to return in a few days time.

ASTRONAUT: Make sure it is ready next time. I am going to Mars and will be back next week.

(Astronaut leaves the shop and in walks Captain KRIK. Sound Effect: space music)

STAR JARS PLAY Script Page 6

STORYTELLER 1: Again the same thing happens. When Old Tom empties out the magic star jars lots of broken bits and pieces fall out.

CAPTAIN KRIK: *(Captain KRIK is furious and shakes his fist at Old Tom)* This is not good enough, Old Tom. I am going to Galaxy Headquarters and will be back next week. Please have my repair ready then.
Beam me up, Paddy!

(Captain KRIK leaves the shop and in walks the Friendly Alien)

STORYTELLER 2: Poor Old Tom. He knows what will happen when he looks in the magic star jar. So, instead, he tells the friendly Alien that his repair is not quite ready because he has been so busy and to return in a few days' time.

(Friendly Alien leaves the shop)

(Old Tom stands in front of the audience shaking his head sadly, his cat Pluto is by his side)

STORYTELLER 1: Everything is going wrong for Old Tom. Unless he finds the rent by next week all will be lost. Added to his troubles the Unfriendly Alien's curse has reversed the magic in the magic star jars and everything is in hundreds of little pieces. What can he do?

(Old Tom sits down in a chair with Pluto beside him)

STORYTELLER 2: It's now Saturday evening, Old Tom and Pluto sit down to eat their cheese supper. They are watching television.
The Interspace Lottery has just started and Old Tom watches with interest as he bought some tickets to try and win some money to pay his rent.

TV ANNOUNCER: And now for this week's Interspace Lottery. There was no overall winner last week, so this week's top prize is an amazing thirty-four million space pounds. WOW! Who will be tonight's lucky winner?
Let's roll the computer and find out those magic numbers.
Ready. Here goes...
The numbers are : one, seven, sixteen, thirty-four, forty-five and forty-nine. If you are out there you lucky winner, give us an Interspace call now.

STAR JARS PLAY Script Page 7

OLD TOM: *(Jumping out of seat and knocking Pluto over)* I've WON! I've WON! *(Helping Pluto up)*. Look, Pluto I have got the winning numbers. We are saved. Let's make that Interspace call.

(Old Tom and Pluto exit stage)

END OF SCENE

SCENE 3

(Old Tom is sitting at his repair table)

STORYTELLER 1: Next morning Old Tom waits for the Unfriendly Alien to visit.

(A loud crash announces the arrival of the Unfriendly Alien)

UNFRIENDLY ALIEN: *(Walking into shop and speaking in a loud roaring voice)*. Well, have you got my rent? I have been looking forward to this moment.

OLD TOM: Yes, here it is. *(handing over a case of money to the Unfriendly Alien)*. There is also another seventeen million space pounds to buy the planet from you. Don't ever bother me again.

UNFRIENDLY ALIEN : How very disappointing. I was hoping to get rid of you.

OLD TOM: Captain KRIK of the Escapade will be here shortly. He is a powerful man and will not think well of your nasty tricks.

UNFRIENDLY ALIEN: Are you threatening me?

OLD TOM: Yes, now go.

UNFRIENDLY ALIEN: You won't always have Captain KRIK on your doorstep!

(Unfriendly Alien laughs nastily) HA, HA, HA, HA.

(Unfriendly Alien leaves the shop)

STORYTELLER 2: Old Tom was very shaken after the visit from the Unfriendly Alien and he was very frightened by the thought that he would probably return another time. However, Old Tom still has his repairs to finish so he returns to his magic star jars and repeats his magic spell.

OLD TOM: APPLE DAPPLE STEW, MAKE EVERYTHING LIKE NEW.

(Old Tom goes and taps all the jars)

STORYTELLER 1: The magic has returned. When all the star jars are emptied out the broken items are repaired. The curse has been lifted.

(Old Tom tips out the repairs and this time they come out of the star jars mended)

STORYTELLER 2: As Old Tom is examining the repaired items the Astronaut, Captain KRIK and the Friendly Alien walk in together to collect their repairs.

(Door Bell rings)

(Tom smiles and hands the repairs back to each of his customers)

CAPTAIN KRIK: Thank you, Old Tom. I have just seen an Alien space ship leave here. Unfortunately as it was gaining speed, the spacecraft exploded. Was he a good customer of yours, Old Tom?

(Old Tom looks surprised and shakes his head at Captain KRIK)

STORYTELLER 1: In his haste to escape from Captain KRIK, the Unfriendly Alien had not strapped on his space seat belt. When the space ship had started to gain warp speed, the Unfriendly Alien had been thrown out of his seat and had fallen heavily on the spaceship's automatic self-destruct button. As a consequence, the ship was blown to pieces and the Unfriendly Alien was destroyed.

STORYTELLER 2: What a relief for Old Tom. He had known the Unfriendly Alien would return to cause him and Pluto more trouble. Now Old Tom can spend the rest of his days living happily on the moon with his cat Pluto and his magic Star Jars.

END

MORE IDEAS FOR THEME PARTIES

Children really enjoy theme parties, planning decorations, games and food ideas that fit into the chosen theme. Most children have particular characters that they like, so the theme will probably be easily found, and it encourages children to join in and use their imaginations.

Listed on the next few pages are just a selection of ideas for a theme party. You and your children can have fun thinking up lots more to choose from.

SHERLOCK HOLMES PARTY

The Adventures of Sherlock Holmes. Design a party around this theme; you can adapt a Sherlock Holmes story for the Play. Try not to make it too long - about 15 minutes is probably enough.

To make the invitations, use the shape of a magnifying glass.

Play lots of detective type games, such as:

- Murder in the Dark, Wink Murder,
- Musical Magnifying Glass,
- Sleeping Detectives,
- Magic Memory Game and so on.

(These are all simple adaptations of the popular games featured in this book).

VAMPIRE PARTY

Boys, in particular, relish a gruesome theme and enter into the spirit of the occasion wholeheartedly! Invitations could be in the form of a bat and games could include ones with a predominantly blood-thirsty theme.

These could include Sleepy Vampires, where players lie on the floor with arms crossed. When the lights are turned off, they awake and roam about making blood curdling noises. When the lights are turned on, they must return to their tombs and the last vampire to lie down drops out of the game. Other games include; Pin the Bat on the Belfry, Musical Tombs, Hunt the Stake, Squeak Vampire Squeak and so on.

For a play, write a vampire story, where perhaps the vampire has become a vegetarian, but although harmless he is still being hunted down by 'Vampire Hunters'. You could perhaps end on a happy note, instead of the usual death of the vampire.

PRINCESS PARTY

Little girls always enjoy the Princess theme and like the opportunity of dressing up in pretty dresses.
To make the invitation, cut out a pretty mask, adding lots of glitter and sparkle, and ask the girls to wear them to the party. Write the party details on the back. Games could include: Musical Thrones, Princess Hoop-La, Pin the Tiara on the Princess, Sleeping Princesses, Musical Stars and so on.

For the play, you could adapt a traditional fairy story such as Cinderella or Sleeping Beauty, perhaps trying to give it a slightly different slant to the original story.